TINA NICHOLS COURY

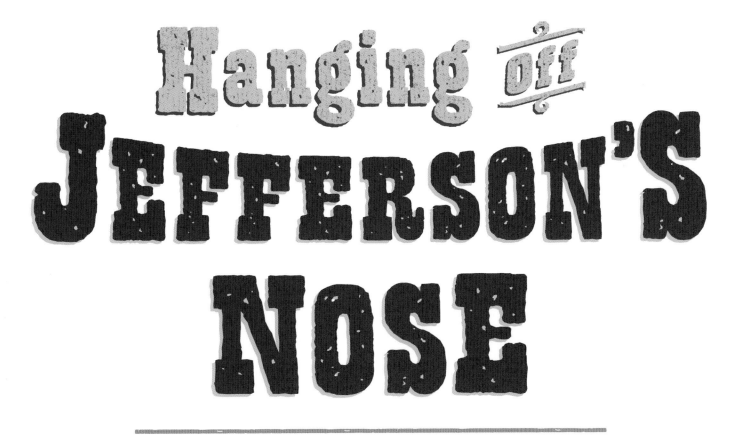

Hanging *off* **JEFFERSON'S NOSE**

GROWING UP ON MOUNT RUSHMORE

Illustrated by SALLY WERN COMPORT

DIAL BOOKS FOR YOUNG READERS An imprint of Penguin Group (USA) Inc.

This book is dedicated to my husband, Al Coury, who inspires me to climb
any mountain no matter how high, and to the kids in my life who keep it
fun, Colt Coury Resch, Ethan Coury, Justin Coury, and Marissa Coury. Also to
Alexis, Barbara, Yuki, and my family, friends, writing buddies, and the SCBWI.

T. N. C.

The labor of these pictures is dedicated to my brother Stephen to whom I am
deeply devoted in life and work and who toils on in the wake of our father,
who lit the spirit of work as redemption.

S. W. C.

ACKNOWLEDGMENTS

The author wishes to thank the National Park Service at Mount Rushmore National Memorial,
especially Judy Olson, Ed Menard, Blaine Kortemeyer; and Debbie Ketel from the Mount Rushmore
History Association. I am grateful to Mary Ellis Borglum Powers and Robin Borglum Carter for their
insightful family stories. Also a big thank you to my agent, Mark McVeigh, and my editor, Steve Meltzer.

DIAL BOOKS FOR YOUNG READERS ✦ A division of Penguin Young Readers Group

Published by The Penguin Group

Penguin Group (USA) Inc., 375 Hudson Street, New York, New York 10014, U.S.A. ✦ Penguin Group (Canada), 90 Eglinton Avenue East, Suite 700, Toronto, Ontario,
M4P 2Y3 Canada (a division of Pearson Penguin Canada Inc.) ✦ Penguin Books Ltd, 80 Strand, London WC2R 0RL, England ✦ Penguin Ireland, 25 St Stephen's Green,
Dublin 2, Ireland (a division of Penguin Books Ltd) ✦ Penguin Group (Australia), 250 Camberwell Road, Camberwell, Victoria 3124, Australia (a division of Pearson
Australia Group Pty Ltd) ✦ Penguin Books India Pvt Ltd, 11 Community Centre, Panchsheel Park, New Delhi—110 017, India ✦ Penguin Group (NZ), 67 Apollo Drive,
Rosedale, Auckland 0632, New Zealand (a division of Pearson New Zealand Ltd) ✦ Penguin Books (South Africa) (Pty) Ltd, 24 Sturdee Avenue, Rosebank, Johannes-
burg 2196, South Africa ✦ Penguin Books Ltd, Registered Offices: 80 Strand, London WC2R 0RL, England

Library of Congress Cataloging-in-Publication Data
Coury, Tina Nichols.
Hanging off Jefferson's nose: growing up on Mount Rushmore/by Tina Nichols Coury; illustrated by Sally Wern Comport. ✦ p. cm.
ISBN 978-0-8037-3731-0 (hardcover)
1. Borglum, Lincoln, 1912-1986—Juvenile literature. 2. Sculptors—United States—Biography—Juvenile literature. 3. Mount Rushmore National Memorial
(S.D.)—Juvenile literature. I. Comport, Sally Wern, ill. II. Title.
NB237.B613C68 2012   730.92—dc23
[B]   2011029968

Published in the United States by Dial Books for Young Readers, a division of Penguin Young Readers Group
345 Hudson Street, New York, New York 10014 ✦ www.penguin.com/youngreaders

The artwork for this book was created from original black-and-white drawings and mixed media layered digital files
that are printed in their hybrid state and final paintings rendered in acrylic and pastel.

Designed by Jason Henry ✦ Text set in Raleigh
Manufactured in Singapore ✦ First Edition
1   3   5   7   9   10   8   6   4   2

IN THE BLACK HILLS OF SOUTH DAKOTA

the giant faces of four presidents gaze down over the prairie. The images of George Washington, Thomas Jefferson, Theodore Roosevelt, and Abraham Lincoln, carved out of the rock of Mount Rushmore, are both a work of art and a memorial for all Americans.

Sculptor Gutzon Borglum designed the monument. But if not for one boy Mount Rushmore might never have been finished.

That boy was the sculptor's son, Lincoln Borglum.

Back in 1920, when Lincoln was eight, the Borglum family moved often. Lincoln's dad was a famous sculptor and the only mountain carver in the world. His work took him all over the country, followed soon after by Lincoln, his mom, and his little sister, Mary Ellis. Whether Gutzon was sculpting a fountain in Connecticut or carving a mountain in Georgia, the Borglum family stayed together.

Always the new kid in class, shy Lincoln found it tough to make friends. He felt more comfortable helping his dad in the art studio. Sometimes Lincoln stood still for hours at a time as a model for his father's statues. Sometimes he swept the art studio clean from corner to corner, and sometimes he watched in wonder as his dad took a lump of clay and shaped it to look like a person.

Lincoln was encouraged to learn many skills at his father's side. When he was ten, he entered a small statue of his own in a contest. When his piece was turned down, he felt bad that he would never be an artist like his dad, but his parents cherished the statue and had it bronzed.

In September of 1924, Lincoln traveled with his dad to South Dakota to find out about a job. Local businessmen met the two in Rapid City and drove them out to a site where they wanted Gutzon to carve huge Wild West figures for a tourist attraction.

Lincoln watched as his dad inspected the rock and declared it was too weak to sculpt. He listened as his dad explained his own idea, to honor the great presidents who had shaped the nation. Later at the café, after dinner, Lincoln learned how his dad planned to carve a mountain into a monument. He watched as Gutzon sketched President George Washington and President Abraham Lincoln right on the tablecloth. The businessmen said the idea was swell, but the waitress looked like she had a bee in her bonnet from staring at that marked up tablecloth.

A year passed. Lincoln and his dad traveled back to South Dakota to find the perfect granite mountain to carve. For three weeks, on horseback, they searched the Black Hills. Lincoln was upset that he was given a pony to ride, because he had ridden horses all his life. But he was too polite to complain. Finally, with help from local guides, they found their mountain—Mount Rushmore.

Only three presidents were planned for the monument, George Washington, Abraham Lincoln, and Thomas Jefferson. Lincoln traveled with his dad to Washington, D.C., and at the White House, he listened as President Coolidge and his dad agreed on the fourth president to be honored—Gutzon's good friend, Theodore Roosevelt.

Thousands of people hiked up from the city of Keystone to Mount Rushmore for the dedication ceremony on August 10, 1927. Bands played, the local Lakota Indians danced, and President Coolidge made a speech. Lincoln held his breath as his dad was lowered over the side and drilled the first hole into the mountain. The carving could now begin.

With money from the federal government and some private donations, Gutzon hired local carpenters, stonecutters, and lumbermen to work as crew. The men built over 500 wood steps to reach the top of Mount Rushmore, where they constructed a small city where they housed tools, cables, and drills. Lincoln was glad not to climb the rickety original steps of chicken wire and branches.

Winch houses were put up to cover the cables that lowered the men over the side. A workshop was constructed to fix any broken machinery. Mount Rushmore was to be carved mostly with dynamite, and a storage shed was built to house the explosives and keep them dry.

At the bottom of the mountain, a small village was built: a blacksmith shop where hundreds of drill bits a day were sharpened; a compressor house to hold compressors that pumped air into the powerful jack-hammers on top, and a bunkhouse where the men could eat and rest.

But most important was an art studio with a massive picture window where Gutzon could view the work on the mountain. Here he sculpted models of the presidents to use as guides for the carving.

South Dakota suited Lincoln. He helped out on Mount Rushmore every chance he got. He mixed the plaster and straw that made up one model, two stories high. Another model was as small as a bread box and molded from a lump of clay. The plan was that all the presidents on Mount Rushmore were to be carved from the waist up. Gutzon also designed a large room behind the heads of the presidents to house the Hall of Records that would hold papers detailing the history of the United States.

The construction of the mountain fascinated Lincoln; he dreamed of becoming an engineer. Then in 1931, Lincoln was accepted to the University of Virginia. He was torn about leaving Mount Rushmore. There was little money in the budget and Lincoln felt he was needed. After a talk with his father, he decided to stay on and work for free.

Now nineteen years old, Lincoln was determined to learn every job on the mountain. He wasn't sure he could do them all, but he wanted to try. The crew, impressed by his hard work, took a shine to Lincoln and trained him in many ways.

As a pointer, he watched as the men took measurements from his father's models and transferred them to the mountain. Soon he was taking measurements by himself.

As a driller, he listened how to precisely use a jackhammer to honeycomb the stone, and then chisel off the rock in between to make a smoother surface.

As a powder man, he learned to plug the drilled holes with wet sand and dynamite. He could explode a slab of granite the size of a house to make Roosevelt's glasses appear or another as small as a hand to make the fold in Washington's scarf.

Twice a day, the crew came down from the top of Mount Rushmore and detonated the charges in the mountain. Lincoln was thrilled to see the faces of the presidents blasted into life.

In 1934, after eighteen months of work, Gutzon discovered the rock under Jefferson's face was unusable. The half-finished image of President Jefferson was blown off the mountain and started again on the other side. Lincoln felt terrible that so much money, time, and work had been wasted.

Through rain, snow, and hail, Gutzon, Lincoln, and the crew worked on. When thunderstorms rolled off the prairie, Lincoln swung under a president's twenty-foot-long nose to protect himself from the lightning. When the temperature dropped, he covered the scaffolding with tarps and lit oil-drum fires to keep the crew warm. When the jackhammers iced shut, he used antifreeze from his car radiator to loosen up the hoses, keeping the drills working in the coldest of weather.

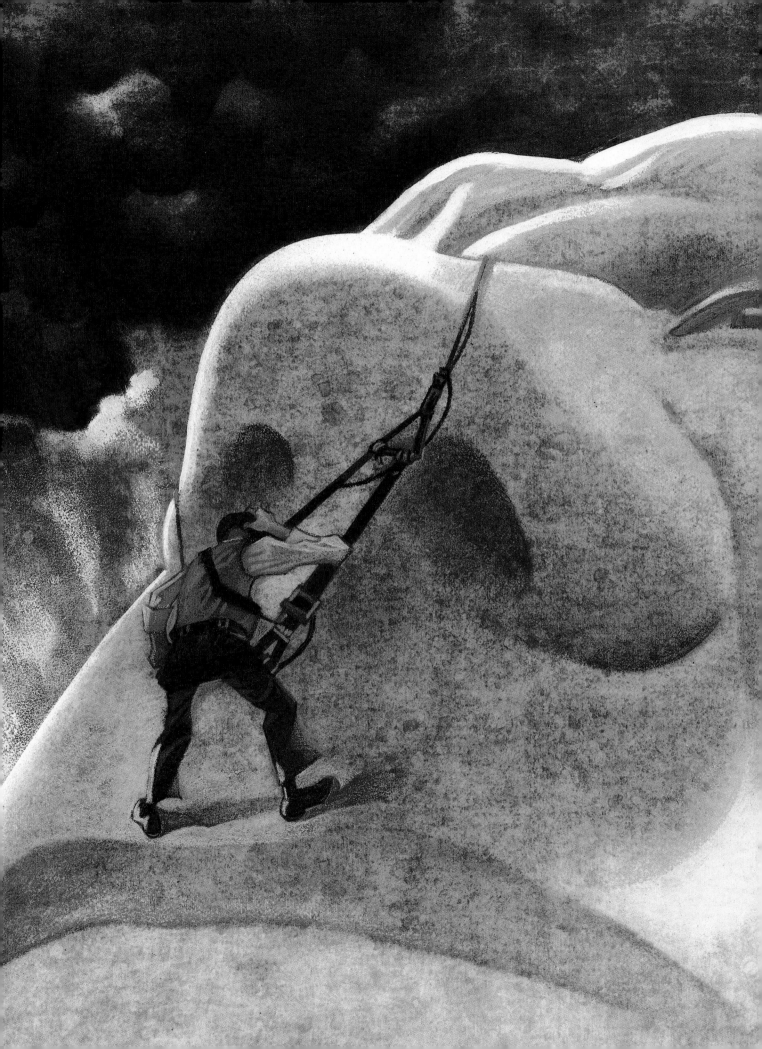

Winters were harsh in the Black Hills. For the Lakota Indians who lived there, food was scarce. The Borglum family helped out often and went so far as to arrange for a buffalo herd to be donated to the tribe. At the powwow to celebrate, the grateful Indians made Lincoln and his dad blood brothers of the Oglala Lakota Tribe at the Pine Ridge Indian Reservation. Lincoln was happy to lend a hand, but dog-tired after dancing all night.

By 1938, Mount Rushmore was four years overdue and Gutzon needed to work on other jobs. He asked Lincoln to become superintendent of all construction. Lincoln hesitated. He would be responsible for the work of hundreds of men. Yet, he understood his father's need for accuracy and hard work. At the age of twenty-six, he agreed to take over the day-to-day operations of carving the mountain.

For the next three years construction continued at a hectic pace. Then in the spring of 1941, Lincoln's father, away on a speaking tour, entered the hospital for minor surgery. There were complications from the operation and on March 6, Gutzon Borglum died. Lincoln was heartbroken. He never had the chance to say good-bye.

Many newspapers said that with Gutzon gone, all work on Mount Rushmore should be shut down immediately and permanently. Even Lincoln might have worried that the papers were right. He was only twenty-nine years old, and his dad had always been there to guide him.

But his family and men encouraged him. The crew signed a petition that asked the Mount Rushmore Commission to name Lincoln head sculptor. The commission agreed. The solid support from the crew touched Lincoln and gave him the courage to finish the job his dad had started. Over the years, he had watched his father deal with cracked granite, bad weather, and lack of money. He had listened to his dad explain the problems with roads, drills, and supplies that never came. Like his father, he had learned to make do with what he had.

With money running short, Lincoln immediately realized that he would not have the resources to finish the Hall of Records behind the heads, as originally planned. He decided to concentrate solely on the faces of the presidents to make the monument look complete.

Through the summer Lincoln and his men worked to detail Abe's beard, narrow Washington's jaw, define Jefferson's collar, and shape Roosevelt's head. They filled cracks in the stone and buffed the presidents' faces smooth and clean. Then, piece by piece, they took down the scaffolding, cables, and the buildings on top and below.

On October 31, 1941, Lincoln gratefully shook the hands of each of the men as they came down the mountain for the last time. It wasn't just his monument; it also belonged to his crew. As he looked up at the completed faces of the presidents glowing in the sunlight, he was proud of his men and the task they had accomplished.

Finally, remembering that the vision of the monument belonged to one man, Lincoln knelt and placed a wreath at the foot of Mount Rushmore in memory of his father, Gutzon Borglum.

Today in the Black Hills of South Dakota, the images of four great presidents tower over the forest, a monumental work of art created by the teamwork, determination, and skill of four hundred men. While it was Gutzon Borglum who designed the great monument on Mount Rushmore, it was his dedicated son, Lincoln, who finished the amazing sculpture for

L INCOLN BORGLUM was appointed Mount Rushmore National Memorial's first superintendent from 1941–1944. After that Lincoln never ventured too far from his beloved Mount Rushmore. He split his time between South Dakota and Texas. Lincoln became a renowned photographer, writer, and sculptor. He wrote books and lectured about the Mount Rushmore for the rest of his life. James Lincoln Borglum died in 1984.

SELECTED BIBLIOGRAPHY

Borglum, James Lincoln. *My Father's Mountain*. Rapid City, SD: Fenwyn Press, 1966.

Casey, Robert J. and Mary Borglum. *Give the Man Room*. Indianapolis: Bobbs-Merrill Company, 1952.

George, Judith. *The Mount Rushmore Story*. New York: Putnam, 1985.

Patrick, Jean L. S. *Face to Face with Mount Rushmore*. Keystone, SC: Mount Rushmore History Association, 2008.

Smith, Rex Alan. *The Carving of Mount Rushmore*. New York: Abbeville Press, 1985.

South Dakota Oral History Project. Interview with Lincoln Borglum, 1983.